Blackbeard: The Life and Legacy of History's Most Famous Pirate

By Charles River Editors

Early 18th century depiction of Blackbeard

About Charles River Editors

Charles River Editors was founded by Harvard and MIT alumni to provide superior editing and original writing services, with the expertise to create digital content for publishers across a vast range of subject matter. In addition to providing original digital content for third party publishers, Charles River Editors republishes civilization's greatest literary works, bringing them to a new generation via ebooks.

Sign up here to receive updates about free books as we publish them, and visit Our Kindle Author Page to browse today's free promotions and our most recently published Kindle titles.

Introduction

1736 engraving depicting Blackbeard

Blackbeard (circa 1680-1718)

"So our Heroe, Captain Teach, assumed the Cognomen of Black-beard, from that large Quantity of Hair, which, like a frightful Meteor, covered his whole Face, and frightened America more than any Comet that has appeared there a long Time. This Beard was black, which he suffered to grow of an extravagant Length; as to Breadth, it came up to his Eyes; he was accustomed to twist it with Ribbons, in small Tails, after the Manner of our Ramilies Wiggs, and turn them about his Ears." - Charles Johnson, *A General History of the Robberies and Murders of the most notorious Pyrates*

It would be an understatement to say that pop culture's perception of piracy and pirates has been primarily influenced by Captain Edward Teach, known to the world as Blackbeard, the most famous pirate of all time. An English pirate who terrorized the high seas near the Carolinas in the early 18th century, a period often referred to as the Golden Age of Piracy, Blackbeard was the gold standard, and in the 300 years since his death he has inspired legends that have spanned books like *Treasure Island*, movies, and even theme park rides.

Of course, like any legendary figure, Blackbeard is remembered today based more on myths than reality. People continue to let their imaginations go when it comes to Blackbeard, picturing a pirate who captured more booty than any other pirate, hid buried treasure, and lit his hair on fire before battle. People have long claimed that his ghost still haunts the Atlantic Ocean, and his contemporaries were so scared of him that they claimed to have seen his headless body swim around his pirate boat three times.

The myths and legends surrounding Blackbeard tend to obscure the life he really lived, but his piracy was also notorious enough to capture headlines during his time. The British Crown put a higher price on his head than any other pirate of the era, and when an author writing under the pseudonym Charles Johnson wrote about Blackbeard in *A General History of the Robberies and Murders of the most notorious Pyrates*, a legend was born.

Blackbeard: The Life and Legacy of History's Most Famous Pirate looks at the mysterious life and death of Blackbeard, separating fact from fiction while analyzing his lasting legacy. Along with pictures depicting Blackbeard and important people, places, and events in his life, you will learn about the famous pirate like you never have before, in no time at all.

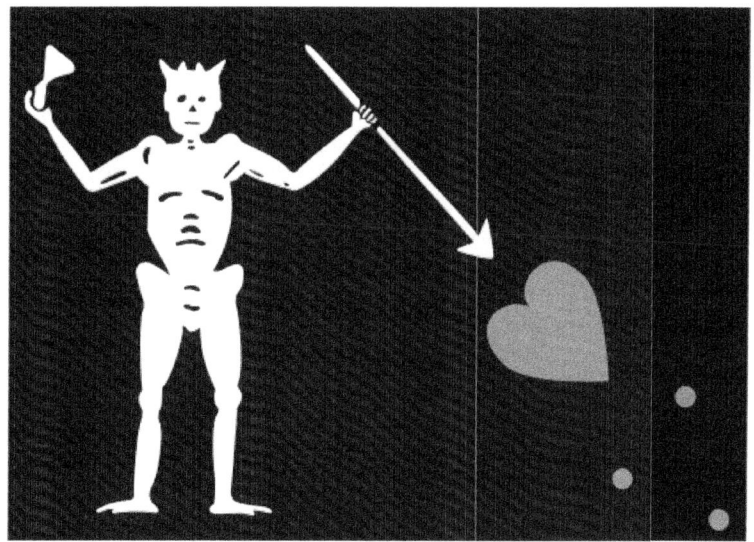

Blackbeard's Pirate Flag, depicting a skeleton spearing a heart while toasting the devil. The infamous flag was designed to intimidate anyone who saw it.

Blackbeard: The Life and Legacy of History's Most Famous Pirate

About Charles River Editors

Introduction

   Chapter 1: The Settlement of the New World

   Chapter 2: Blackbeard's Early Life

   Chapter 3: Becoming a Pirate

   Chapter 4: Becoming Blackbeard

   Chapter 5: The Legend and the Fleet Grows

   Chapter 6: The Return of Blackbeard

   Chapter 7: Blackbeard's Legacy

   Blackbeard's Entry in *A General History of the Pyrates*

Chapter 1: The Settlement of the New World

Though Blackbeard's origins are not very directly in the hands of Christopher Columbus, the famous explorer played an important role in Blackbeard's future. In 1492, of course, Columbus historic voyage across the Atlantic landed him in the West Indies. Columbus had discovered a New World that had been dormant in the Western imagination for nearly half a millenium. Not since the Norseman Leif Ericson landed in Newfoundland had a European ventured as far across the Atlantic.

Columbus' "discovery" set off a wave of interest in the New World, particularly from the Iberian Peninsula. Spaniards and the Portuguese rapidly raced to take away the riches that were present in Columbus' New World. Spanish colonization quickly took the lead, and just a year later permanent Spanish settlement began at Hispaniola in the year 1493. By 1511, Cuba was conquered by the Spanish, and much of the Caribbean was in the Empire's control.

By 1513, the Spanish were off the islands and on the American mainland. That year, Ponce De Leon conquered modern-day Florida, adding land to the empire, and less than a decade later, in 1521, Hernan Cortes completed his conquest of the Aztec Empire in modern-day Mexico, adding a huge swath of South and Central America to the Spanish Empire.

By the mid-1500's, the Spanish controlled much of the New World, with the Portuguese controlling small parts of it in the southern periphery. Quickly, though, other nations - namely, France and England - were taking note of Spain's rapid expansion. They, too, wanted a piece of the world's newest prize.

John Cabot was much more directly related to Blackbeard's future. Cabot, another Italian, was commissioned by the English crown to explore parts of the New World, specifically in North America. Cabot's dictate was to explore the north of the North American continent, and he thought, based on preliminary maps, that the distance between England and the New World was significantly shorter than that between Spain and its overseas possessions. Cabot thought the trip would be much easier, faster and more economical, and thus went to England first, and, to his surprise, quickly received a positive response.

Shortly thereafter, Cabot departed the Old World from Bistol, England, and in June 1497, the English voyage made landfall on the coast of modern-day Newfoundland. Cabot's exact landing spot remains uncertain, but Canada and the United Kingdom both recognize Cape Bonavista in Newfoundland as the "official" location of Cabot's landing.

Portrait of Cabot

Upon return to England, Cabot went directly to see the King and tell him of his discoveries, and the King gave him a significant sum, while also asking Cabot to conduct a second mission to North America to further explore the region.

John Cabot had found what was believed to be the fabled Northwest Passage, and throughout England the public clamored for the establishment of an English colonial empire. The recent Protestant Reformation had made enemies of England and Spain, with England controlled by Protestants and Spain by Catholics. England could no longer be so far behind its Spanish counterparts in the race to dominate the New World.

The origins of the English Empire lie squarely with Queen Elizabeth I. Her reign was marked by calmness at home: the Protestant Reformation, having ravaged England's political stability for decades, was now mostly settled. Some groups, namely the Separatists and the Puritans, remained dissatisfied, but they were for the most part on the periphery of English life.

Throughout the 1500's, England made claims to various territories across the New World, but did little to actively exploit them. In 1576, Baffin Island was claimed for England by Sir Francis Drake. Later, Elizabeth Island off Cape Horn was claimed. In 1583, St. John's on modern-day Newfoundland was claimed. The expansion was rapid but remained insignificant; England "claimed" multiple islands and locations, but it failed to either settle on them or actively take resources away, as the Spanish and Portuguese had been doing for nearly a century.

By 1584, it was apparent to Queen Elizabeth that her colonial ventures were going nowhere, and compared to Spain her nation was far behind. That year, she asked Sir Walter Raleigh to establish a colony in North America that would be named, in her honor, Virginia. He would have seven years to complete the mission or otherwise lose his charter.

Raleigh did not want to go on his own, however. He sent people, led by his distant cousins, to establish a colony in modern-day North Carolina named the Roanoke Colony. The colony, however, was riddled with problems, especially the fact that it was unable to protect and fend for itself thanks to tense relations with local Native Americans. The colony famously and mysteriously failed, coming to be known as the "Lost Colony", but other ventures were more successful. In the early 1600's, the colony of Bermuda was established on an island in the Atlantic. Jamestown was perhaps the most successful, founded in 1607 in the Virginia colony. It was the first permanent settlement in North America.

Later attempts to colonize took a different form. The earlier settlements were "proprietary" ventures, meaning they intended to make financial gains for the Crown, but later settlements, such as the Plymouth Colony and Massachusetts Bay, were more autonomous in their settlement. Though they benefited England, they also enjoyed a measure of their own sovereignty.

The area Blackbeard would later terrify the most - the Carolinas - was settled rather late in the history of English colonization. Whereas Virginia was settled in 1607, Massachusetts in 1620, and parts of Canada even in the late 1500's, the Carolina's were not settled until the 1660's. This was due in part to Spanish imperial claims over the region, which inhibited English expansion, but in 1663 Parliament issued a charter to a series of noblemen to establish the Province of Carolina south of Virginia. Not until 1729 was the area split into a South Carolina and a North Carolina.

A decade earlier, the Albemarle settlements became the first English settlement in the region. Immigrants from New England, Virginia, and Bermuda were responsible for settling the coastal area, but the settlement of the Carolinas remained coastal, with almost no inland settlement. This was unlike New England and Virginia, where settlement moved westward more quickly.

The government of the Province of Carolina was uniquely dictatorial among the English colonies of North America. Rather than have a popularly-elected colonial government, like Massachusetts and Virginia, Carolina was governed by a council of Lord Proprietors who appointed all the officials of government themselves. They were also particularly independent of the King himself and were able to govern without much intervention from London. By the time Blackbeard would wreak havoc across the Carolinas, this remained the method of governance in the two colonies. Lords appointed the officials of government, and almost no democratic rule existed. This made corruption rampant and enabled Blackbeard and other pirates to use the Carolinas as safe havens, even as the citizens of the colonies were displaced by the piracy.

The colonists upset with pirates could rely on one powerful ally. Around the time that the English colonies were settled in the New World, the country's navy was becoming the world's most powerful naval force. In the late 16th century, the Royal Navy managed to successfully defend against the invasion of the Spanish Armada by the Catholic King of Spain, who hoped to overthrow Queen Elizabeth and end Protestantism in England.

England's naval rise, however, caused conflict with other countries, especially the Netherlands. In the 1640's England passed a law known as the Navigation Acts, which required that all shipments to and from England were to be carried on English ships. The Dutch, however, were unhappy with this law, and declared war on England. The resulting First Anglo-Dutch War lasted from 1652 until 1654, but the war was inconclusive. A decade later, the Second Anglo-Dutch War erupted but again achieved largely inconclusive results. England's naval superiority in the Atlantic remained unmatched, enabling it to capture numerous critical locations and to ship ever more people overseas. This contrasted somewhat with the Spanish method of colonization, where a relatively few number of bureaucrats and crew moved to the New World and returned with gold and other resources to Spain.

At the same time, English expansion into the islands of the New World made the area somewhat lawless. Many nations from Europe attempted to gain control of the various islands of the Caribbean, leading to competition that mostly took place on the seas, leaving no single nation able to enforce law and order in the area. Naturally, piracy exploded in this environment, with many pirates igniting fear across the warm tropical seas of the middle Atlantic.

Chapter 2: Blackbeard's Early Life

Perhaps not surprisingly, the elusive Blackbeard's origins and early years are relatively unknown, and the mysterious beginnings added to the intrigue surrounding the subsequently famous English pirate. Though he is commonly referred to as Edward Teach, the name used most often today, there have historically been several other spellings of his last name, including Thatch, Thach, Thache, Thack, Tack, Thatche and Theach. It was also possible that Blackbeard intentionally obscured his real name to spare his family and anyone else who was unfortunate enough to have the same last name.

 Though some undocumented accounts claim he was born in Jamaica, the place from which he would eventually launch his career on the seas, Blackbeard was more likely born in England, probably near Bristol, around the year 1680. Bristol is a port city in an inlet in the southeastern region of England and was an important one in the development of English colonization, since it was the port from which many early colonists departed. Bristol was also a center in the triangular slave trade route that now dominated the Atlantic Ocean, so as a young boy he would have likely seen this type of commerce developing in his home town, and he may have developed a fervent interest in the New World that was making his town and its people rich.

 Shipping and the navy thus dominated the world in which the future pirate lived, and contemporary evidence suggests that he could read and write, meaning he at least came from a relatively modest family who could afford education. At the same time, the highest echelons of the shipping and naval trade were unavailable to most English save for the wealthy. It's assumed that these echelons were unavailable to the young boy in Bristol.

 Because so little is known about his early life, it remains unclear when and why he left Bristol. The lack of opportunity available to the young man may have led him to go rogue and engage in piracy. Alternatively, the young boy may have taken haven in the Royal Navy, which was growing and was thus not particularly selective when it came to recruiting. It's this route - the Navy - where many think Edward Teach got his first experiences in shipping and seafaring, and it is presumed that he got these first experiences during Queen Anne's War.

 The War of Spanish Succession broke out in the year 1702, and by then Spain was considered by many to be a declining power. It had a large territorial domain, but its technological advances over the past two centuries were few compared to its counterparts in Britain, France and even Italy. However, in 1702, the inheritance of the Spanish crown became uncertain because a sickly child had inherited the throne. The Hapsburgs of central Europe were now competing with the Bourbons of France, with both families claiming the right to rule all of Spain's realms.

 Britain, meanwhile, preferred that the Spanish realms be ruled in a dispersed manner by multiple related monarchs; their unification into one unit was considered a threat. Other countries, including the Netherlands, Portugal, the remains of the Holy Roman Empire, and even some Spaniards loyal to King Charles, agreed with Britain. France, Spain and Bavaria wanted unification, because they would all be united together. The two sides eventually went to war.

 In Europe, the war was called the War of Spanish Succession, since that was the substance of the war, but in North America it was known as Queen Anne's War. Each of the major belligerents - Spain, France and England - controlled critical pieces of North America, ultimately sucking them in despite the fact they were far removed from European thrones. In North America, the hostilities focused principally on various border disputes, and the Native Americans in the region were also actively involved in the development of the conflict.

During the war, another significant change took place. The English colonists in North America were no longer English - in 1707, with the Act of Union, they became British. That year, Queen Anne, Queen of England, Scotland and Ireland, which she ruled separately, had her three Parliaments agree to unite their countries into a single political unit - the United Kingdom of Great Britain and Ireland. Ironically, this type of political union was precisely what the Queen was fighting against in France and Spain

In North America, France and Spain allied against Britain, and each had Native American allies. The war was largely fought along territorial borders - in Spanish Florida, in New England, especially in modern-day Maine and in Southern Canada, and in Newfoundland, where a border dispute existed between France and England, until the war ended with the Treaty of Utrecht in 1713. France ceded parts of the Hudson Bay, Maine and Newfoundland to England, positive results for Britain's North American colonies.

In the famous pirate history written in the mid-18th century by someone using the pseudonym "Captain Charles Johnson", Teach is credited with being a privateer during Queen Anne's War, operating in and around Jamaica. Being a privateer was, in some sense, legalized piracy; a privateer was not a member of the Royal Navy but instead owned his own private ship and received a contract (called a letter of marquee) from the government to attack enemy ships during a time of war. This allowed the marque-awarding government to place undercover ships out to war. It also, however, made the enemy wary of anything the opposing belligerent owned, and caused many private ships to be enveloped in the war, even the kinds of merchant ships that posed no threat and were essentially civilian targets.

The point of a privateer was either to augment a small government navy - which was not Britain's purpose - or to disrupt an enemy who was heavily dependent on trade. Spain's Empire was larger and more exploitive; the country reaped enormous fortunes out of North America while the Britain, meanwhile, had established small and dwindling societies across the Atlantic coast. Moreover, the British colonies were all relatively independent and did little to support Britain other than provide it with usable military territory. Britain thus made up the difference by having privateers steal from Spanish ships during Queen Anne's War.

The line between a privateer and a pirate was often vague. For practical purposes, there was no apparent difference, other than that a privateer was legally sanctioned by a government while a pirate was often a freerider independent of any larger organization. When it came to day-to-day activities, however, the aim of the privateer was the same as that of the pirate: to find treasure and to steal it.

It was presumably in this environment that Edward Teach first gained his knowledge of piracy and the sea. He is alleged to have been a very successful privateer throughout the duration of Queen Anne's War and was responsible for sacking and pillaging Spanish ships throughout the Southern Atlantic and the Caribbean. In addition to being successful at it, Edward Teach also took a liking to it, to the extent that the end of the war left Teach jobless and without a purpose. Captain Charles Johnson wrote that he "had often distinguished himself for his uncommon boldness and personal courage", and now he would have to find a new way of utilizing it.

Chapter 3: Becoming a Pirate

Depiction of Blackbeard in Johnsons's history of the pirates

Queen Anne's War ended in 1713, but contemporary histories state that Teach did not get into piracy until 1716. It is believed that he spent the next 3 years in New Providence, a once uninhabited island that privateer-turned-pirate Henry Jennings helped turn into a lawless trading town consisting mostly of pirates and other traders. The island was the perfect spot for pirates because it was close to the commercial shipping lanes near Florida Strait, it was big enough for dozens of ships to dock, and it was shallow enough that the various imperial navies of the European empires had to avoid giving chase too far. Author George Woodbury noted New Providence was " a place of temporary sojourn and refreshment for a literally floating population," and that its residents "were the piratical camp followers, the traders, and the hangers-on…"

After the war, Teach decided to stick with the seafaring ways he had learned over the past few years, and now that he was no longer sanctioned by the British government, his conversion from privateer to pirate was complete. Teach got his start in piracy with Benjamin Hornigold, whose career in piracy also began immediately after the end of Queen Anne's War. Hornigold was a pirate leader who had been instrumental in helping implement what became known as a pirate republic in the West Indies, and as an Englishman he was concerned that Spanish boats would continue privateering even after the war. At the very least, he used that as a justification to begin attacking ships in and around the Bahamas, stealing resources and ships in high quantities. In the process, he acquired enough ships, including sloops and merchant vessels, to command an entire fleet of pirates, menacing the Caribbean.

Illustration depicting Hornigold

Hornigold's primary and most important ship was the *Ranger*, a well-armed vessel that was the most impressive and feared ship in the region during the period, and his second-in-command was none other than Edward Teach, who had command of the second largest sloop in Hornigold's fleet. It's still unclear how Teach managed to snag such a vaunted position; according to Charles Johnson's history, "[Teach] was never raised to any Command, till he went a-pyrating, which I think was at the latter End of the Year 1716, when Captain Benjamin Hornigold put him into a Sloop that he had made Prize of, and with whom he continued in Consortship till a little while before Hornigold surrendered." Another anti-piracy report claimed that Teach was in command of "a sloop 6 gunns [sic] and about 70 men".

Teach's piracy truly took off in 1717, beginning with Hornigold's fleet raiding a series of Spanish and Portuguese ships throughout the Caribbean, during which they stole tons of flour and white wine and later sold it at higher prices. While Blackbeard would gain a reputation for ferocity, and pirates would become known for making their prisoners walk the plank, the crews of the ships captured by Hornigold's fleet that spring were safely released. But he and his crew did fit one pirate stereotype; during their piracy, Teach and his crew became quite fond of the liquor they stole from other ships, especially Madeira wine, and their affinity for it became so strong that when they captured a ship called *Betty* in late September 1717, they only took the Madeira wine onboard before scuttling the ship with its crew and cargo.

That same month, Hornigold's fleet met with the notorious pirate Stede Bonnet, a well-to-do young man in the New World who decided to become a pirate in 1717 after marital troubles with his wife popped up. Known as "The Gentleman Pirate", Bonnet was ambitious but inexperienced, and though he and his crew had some successes capturing boats that year, his crew began pining for better leadership. Moreover, Bonnet had been seriously injured while attacking a Spanish ship. Thus, in September 1717, Bonnet acquiesced to letting Teach come onboard to command his ship, named *Revenge*, and with that Hornigold's fleet had added yet another ship. Johnson profiled Bonnet in his pirate history and explained how Bonnet became part of the pirate fleet:

"THE Major was a Gentleman of good Reputation in the Island of Barbadoes, was Master of a plentiful Fortune, and had the Advantage of a liberal Education. He had the least Temptation of any Man to follow such a Course of Life, from the Condition of his Circumstances. It was very surprizing to every one, to hear of the Major's Enterprize, in the Island were he liv'd; and as he was generally esteem'd and honoured, before he broke out into open Acts of Pyracy, so he was afterwards rather pitty'd than condemned, by those that were acquainted with him, believing that this Humour of going a pyrating, proceeded from a Disorder in his Mind, which had been but too visible in him, some Time before this wicked Undertaking; and which is said to have been occasioned by some Discomforts he found in a married State; be that as it will, the Major was but ill qualify'd for the Business, as not understanding maritime Affairs.

The Major was no Sailor as was said before, and therefore had been obliged to yield to many Things that were imposed on him, during their Undertaking, for want of a competent Knowledge in maritime Affairs; at length happening to fall in Company with another Pyrate, one Edward Teach, (who for his remarkable black ugly Beard, was more commonly called Black-Beard:) This Fellow was a good Sailor, but a most cruel hardened Villain, bold and daring to the last Degree, and would not stick at the perpetrating the most abominable Wickedness imaginable; for which he was made Chief of that execrable Gang, that it might be said that his Post was not unduly filled, Black-beard being truly the Superior in Roguery, of all the Company, as has been already related.

To him Bonnet's Crew joined in Consortship, and Bonnet himself was laid aside, notwithstanding the Sloop was his own; he went aboard Black-beard's Ship, not concerning himself with any of their Affairs."

Engraving depicting Stede Bonnet

One of the ways pirates of the era justified their piracy was by casting it as a patriotic venture that helped the Mother Country. Thus, Hornigold, an Englishman, refrained from attacking British ships, thinking that by doing so it would ultimately allow the pirate to be considered a privateer. It's just as likely that it intended to soothe Hornigold's conscience as he and his men continued attacking Spanish, French and Portugese ships. Attacking a British ship, however, would permanently leave him unable to gain legal protection if it was ever granted, so he continued to choose not to go after British boats.

His crew, however, thought otherwise. Aware of their status as pirates, the crew figured they may as well attack any ship carrying valuable cargo if possible, and they voted in late 1717 to begin attacking all ships, including those stationed out of Britain. It's unclear what if any role Teach played, or what position he advocated, but since Hornigold still opposed the idea, his crew was determined not to continue with him. Hornigold opted to head back to Jamaica, taking the *Ranger* with him. The fleet was now down to the *Revenge* and the sloop that Teach commanded before moving onto the *Revenge*.

Teach and Hornigold would never see each other again.

Chapter 4: Becoming Blackbeard

Teach's reaction to Hornigold's retirement from piracy is not entirely known, but its clear that he had absolutely no qualms about continuing his piracy. If anything, he became even more ambitious.

On November 28, 1717, Teach's *Revenge* and the other sloop conducted a daring attack against the slave ship *La Concorde* off the coast of French-controlled Saint Vincent. *La Concorde* had actually been a British frigate originally named *The Concord*, and it was a frigate equipped for warfare. It had undergone some adaptations that made it even better equipped for fighting during Queen Anne's War, but at the time it encountered Teach, dozens of crewmembers were ill with scurvy and dysentery.

Still, *La Concorde* was carrying a large cargo of slaves just recently obtained in Africa and was hardly willing to be taken without a fight, so when Teach's small fleet approached, *La Concorde* sailed into position to deliver a broadside of its own. Both ships fired at each other, killing an untold number on each side, but after firing a second volley Teach and his crew managed to subdue *La Concorde* and its crew. Instead of sailing to its destination as intended, the pirates commanded *La Concorde* to the Grenadines and dropped off its crew and cargo on the large island of Bequia.

The ship itself was another story. After all, it wasn't every day that pirates had a chance to commandeer a frigate, which posed a mortal danger to their own sloops as opposed to typical merchant vessels. The pirates had grand designs for *La Concorde*, and they began outfitting it with the intention of converting it for themselves. Once they were finished, Teach and his crew now had a new flagship, and *La Concorde* became *Queen Anne's Revenge*. Meanwhile, the French crew originally commanding *La Concorde* were given the pirates' smaller sloop, which they appropriately renamed *Mauvais Rencontre* (French for "Bad Encounter").

According to Charles Johnson, Teach had been given command of Queen Anne's Revenge with Hornigold's consent, suggesting that Hornigold had not yet been voted out and sent into retirement. Johnson wrote, "After cleaning on the Coast of Virginia, they returned to the West-Indies, and in the Latitude of 24, made Prize of a large French Guiney Man, bound to Martinico, which by Hornigold's Consent, Teach went aboard of as Captain, and took a Cruize in her; Hornigold returned with his Sloop to Providence, where, at the Arrival of Captain Rogers, the Governor, he surrendered to Mercy, pursuant to the King's Proclamation." However, it's widely believed that the attack on *La Concorde* was conducted only by Teach and his crew, suggesting that Hornigold was already out of the picture.

Whatever the case, the pirates now had a ship that was ideal for piracy. *Queen Anne's Revenge* was built as a frigate, a ship originally equipped for war, but by being converted to use for the slave trade it was also well-equipped to transport stolen goods. Thus, *Queen Anne's Revenge* could serve dual purposes, precisely what the pirates needed to destroy other ships and transport stolen goods.

18th century depiction of *Queen Anne's Revenge*

When Teach and his crew stole the ship, *La Concorde* was armed with about 14 guns, but *Queen Anne's Revenge* was armed with 40 guns, making it capable of attacking just about anything it wanted. It seemingly took no time for the pirates to utilize their new firepower; they attacked a big merchant ship called *Great Allen* near Saint Vincent, around where they captured *La Concorde*, and they won the battle against the well-equipped ship. The pirates ransacked the *Great Allen*, jettisoned the crew near shore, and burned and scuttled the vessel near the shore. The daring attack even found its way into newspapers as far north as Boston; the Boston News Letter noted the pirates had a "French ship of 32 Guns, a Briganteen of 10 guns and a Sloop of 12 guns." It's unclear when the pirates had acquired the Briganteen, but its addition meant Teach was in command of three ships and about 150 pirates.

In early December, the pirates tried their hand against the *Margaret* near the island of Anguilla in the British Virgin Islands, eventually commandeering the vessel. As Teach and his crew began stealing the goods from the *Margaret*, they forced the ship's crew to sit in captivity for about eight hours, and the ship's captain, Henry Bostock, was held aboard the *Queen Anne's Revenge*. After taking all the goods they wanted, the pirates let Bostock and his crew take back command of the *Margaret* and depart aboard their ship.

Whether Teach knew it or not, that was not the end of the matter, because Bostock went looking for some sort of justice. When he returned to his base on Saint Christopher Island, Bostock signed an affidavit with the Governor about the matter, during which he described Teach, the *Queen Anne's Revenge*, and more. Bostock noted that the pirate leader was a "tall spare man with a very black beard which he wore very long", the first contemporary reference to take note of Teach's most noticeable feature. Bostock claimed the pirates numbered 300, and the fleet consisted of a sloop and a large French guineaman with three dozen cannons. Bostock also noted that the flagship (*Queen Anne's Revenge*) contained a bunch of valuable (and presumably stolen) goods, including thousands of pounds of gold and silver. And whether it was true or just bluster intending to intimidate Bostock, Teach had told him the pirates had ransacked several other ships and intended to head to Hispaniola and ambush Spanish vessels.

Bostock's account has led some scholars to believe that Teach and his crew were responsible for attacking the *Monserrat Merchant*, which claimed to have encountered two ships and a sloop captained by men named Kentish and Edwards on November 30. Captain Edwards was an alias commonly used by Stede Bonnet, who was part of Teach's crew.

With Bostock having noted his long black beard, Teach shortly became known as Blackbeard, and descriptions of his beard became even more colorful over time. Several accounts described him as tying small ribbons of different colors into his beard, braiding it all the way around his ears, and in some cases lighting it on fire. Captain Johnson simply described Blackbeard as "a figure that imagination cannot form an idea of a fury from hell to look more frightful." The tall pirate was also described as wearing dark clothes, large boots, a big hat, and a colorful silk or velvet coat, and in battle Johnson wrote that he wore "a sling over his shoulders, with three brace of pistols, hanging in holsters like bandoliers; and stuck lighted matches under his hat." In essence, Blackbeard cut the very image that people today think of when picturing the pirates of this Golden Age of Piracy, and it's obvious that Blackbeard realized there was something to gain by appearing as intimidating as possible.

By the spring of 1718, the British government was referring to Teach as Blackbeard, and with that reports and accounts of his actions used the name Blackbeard as well. In conjunction, *Queen*

Anne's Revenge became the well-known flagship for Blackbeard and became synonymous with the terror associated with his fleet. The capture of *La Concorde* and its conversion into *Queen Anne's Revenge* may even have induced Blackbeard to grow out his famous beard. It's been suggested that prior to acquiring *Queen Anne's Revenge*, Blackbeard did not keep a long straggly beard but only started growing a fearsome beard once he had captured the fearsome frigate.

The more the pirate plundered, the more famous Blackbeard became across all of the British colonies in North America. Boston area newspapers followed Blackbeard's activities thereafter, even though he posed no threat to Boston, and naturally he garnered press in the Southern colonies, particularly around the coast of the Carolinas, which feared the pirate's advance into its waters. But like any legendary outlaw, Blackbeard was romanticized by some of the British colonists, who both feared the pirate and reveled in the colorful accounts of his conquests.

Chapter 5: The Legend and the Fleet Grows

The life of a pirate was not easy, and their fates were always up in the air, whether it was contracting a deadly illness while at sea or being captured and sent to the gallows. But in 1718 there were a couple of opportunities for pirates. In North America, Britain's Southern colonies braced themselves for a wave of piracy, but some residing there were not necessarily unhappy about such a wave, instead viewing it as a way to reap its profits. Meanwhile, the British government back in London began floating the possibility of combating piracy by offering pirates pardons that would offer them a way out of the lifestyle without being hanged. Pirates like Hornigold would choose one route, but others like Blackbeard would go the other way.

In February 1718, the Royal Navy was on the lookout for Blackbeard, and on February 6 the HMS *Scarborough* engaged a "Pyrate Ship of 36 Guns and 250 men, and a Sloop of 10 Guns and 100 men were Said to be Cruizing amongst the Leeward Islands". It is presumed this was Blackbeard's fleet. The *Scarborough*'s captain linked up with HMS *Seaford* to track and attack the pirates, but the *Queen Anne's Revenge* was so well-manned and well-armed that it could now go toe to toe with Britain's naval ships. Charles Johnson wrote, "A few Days after, Teach fell in with the Scarborogh Man of War, of 30 Guns, who engaged him for some Hours; but she finding the Pyrate well mann'd, and having tried her strength, gave over the Engagement, and returned to Barbadoes, the Place of her Station; and Teach sailed towards the Spanish America." The captain of the *Scarborough* reported that they last saw the pirate fleet headed "down the North side of Hispaniola", which would make sense given what Blackbeard had said to Bostock while capturing the *Margaret*.

According to Bostock's affidavit, Blackbeard was aware that authorities in London were planning to offer pardons to those pirates who would accept them, but in the early months of 1718, the swashbuckling pirate instead took huge strides to expand his crew and his fleet. While the Royal Navy and the British colonies in North America were on the lookout, Blackbeard sailed toward Central America in March, where his crew managed to stop a ship called the *Adventure* near Belize. But rather than sack the ship the pirates convinced the crew and the ship to join their fleet, possibly because the two pirate vessels themselves were taking on water and not fit for fighting. Charles Johnson credited the success to the intimidating appearance of the *Queen Anne's Revenge* and its famous flag: "At Turniff ten Leagues short of the Bay of Honduras, the Pyrates took in fresh Water; and while they were at an Anchor there, they saw a Sloop coming in, whereupon, Richards in the Sloop called the Revenge, slipped his Cable, and run out to meet her; who upon seeing the black Flag hoisted, struck his Sail and came to, under the Stern of Teach the Commadore. She was called the Adventure, from Jamaica, David Harriot Master. They took him and his Men aboard the great Ship, and sent a Number of other Hands with Israel Hands, Master of Teach's Ship, to Man the Sloop for the pyratical Account."

Whatever the reasons, David Harriot, an experienced ship captain, joined Blackbeard in his mission to destroy ships across the Caribbean, and the new group moved toward the Bay of Honduras, where they commandeered another ship and four sloops, adding them to Blackbeard's growing flotilla. Charles Johnson provided the details of Blackbeard's movements and additions during these early months:

"The 9th of April, they weighed from Turniff, having lain there about a Week, and sailed to the Bay, where they found a Ship and four Sloops, three of the latter belonged to Jonathan Bernard, of Jamaica, and the other to Captain James; the Ship was of Boston, called the Protestant Cæsar, Captain Wyar Commander. Teach hoisted his Black Colours, and fired a Gun, upon which Captain Wyar and all his Men, left their Ship, and got ashore in their Boat. Teach's Quarter-Master, and eight of his Crew, took Possession of Wyar's Ship, and Richards secured all the Sloops, one of which they burnt out of spight to the Owner; the Protestant Cæsar they also burnt, after they had plundered her, because she belonged to Boston, where some Men had been hanged for Pyracy; and the three Sloops belonging to Bernard they let go.

From hence the Rovers sailed to Turkill, and then to the Grand Caimanes, a small Island about thirty Leagues to the Westward of Jamaica, where they took a small Turtler, and so to the Havana, and from thence to the Bahama Wrecks, and from the Bahama Wrecks, they sailed to Carolina, taking a Brigantine and two Sloops in their Way."

With this sizable fleet, Blackbeard decided upon a rather ambitious objective: to blockade the port of Charleston, South Carolina. The early history of Charleston was riddled with problems. First, it was disputed territory between England and Spain. More importantly, it was under almost constant attack from nearby Native Americans hoping to avoid the fate of their northern counterparts, who had all but ceased to exist as a result of colonial expansion. But at the same time, its location ensured that it remained an important trading center between the English colonies in North America and the colonies in the islands of the Atlantic.

In May 1718, Blackbeard decided to blockade the famous port, which sounds suicidal until taking into account that the townspeople were busy fighting Native Americans on land and the port could not afford to have guard ships, leaving it vulnerable to attack. For about a week, Blackbeard and his crew stopped each and every ship that tried to enter or leave the harbor, detaining all the crew aboard their ships and plundering their goods. But this created another problem; with so many people onboard, some in poor condition, the pirates needed medical supplies. According to Johnson, Blackbeard had some of his pirates take one of the prisoners to the colony's leaders and demand medical supplies, threatening to murder every prisoner they had taken and deliver their severed heads to the Governor if their demand was not met. The pirate "ambassadors" also promised that Blackbeard would murder the prisoners if the colony did not allow them to return to their fleet. As a result, the pirates "walk'd the Streets publickly, in the Sight of all People, who were fired with the utmost Indignation, looking upon them as Robbers and Murtherers, and particularly the Authors of their Wrongs and Oppressions, but durst not so much as think of executing their Revenge, for fear of bringing more Calamities upon themselves, and so they were forced to let the Villains pass with Impunity."

Thanks to the pirate ambassadors' fondness for drinking, things nearly went awry even after the Governor agreed to the demands. The pirates were given a couple of days to collect the necessary medical supplies, but when they did not return, Blackbeard got nervous and moved his fleet and the detained ships to within sight of land, spreading even more panic. Eventually the prisoner they had taken along, a man Johnson called "Mr. Marks", returned and explained that the pirates had spent the last several days in Charleston getting drunk. Once the medical supplies and the pirates returned, Blackbeard released the ships and their crews, but without their goods.

After leaving Charleston, Blackbeard and his crew navigated north to an area known as Beaufort's Inlet in North Carolina, a move made primarily because they had gotten word that the British were sending a fleet of men-of-war to go after pirates across the West Indies and remove them from power. The British fleet was commanded by the famous privateer Woodes Rogers.

Woodes Rogers (right) receives a map of New Providence

In the process of trying to sail north, Blackbeard ran his prized flag ship aground in Beaufort Inlet. It has long been assumed that the *Queen Anne's Revenge* intended to hit sand and come to a stop but instead hit rock, cracking its main-mast and damaging much of its critical timbers. The ship began to take on water and would no longer be able to serve as Blackbeard's main base of operations. In an attempt to save the ship, Blackbeard ordered that numerous sloops throw ropes across the boat and try to pull it off the sandbar, but that only caused more problems because the sloops were destroyed in the process.

Scholars and other interested individuals have long tried to pinpoint the location where the *Queen Anne's Revenge* ran aground, and in the process there has been speculation that Blackbeard did it intentionally. David Herriot, captain of the *Adventure*, wrote that "the said Thatch's ship *Queen Anne's Revenge* run a-ground off of the Bar of Topsail-Inlet." Herriot also reported that the *Adventure* "run a-ground likewise about Gun-shot from the said Thatch". Captain Ellis Brand, commanding the HMS *Lyme*, reported in a letter to the Lords of Admiralty in July 1718, "On the 10th of June or thereabouts a large pyrate Ship of forty Guns with three Sloops in her company came upon the coast of North carolina ware they endeavour'd To goe in to a harbour, call'd Topsail Inlett, the Ship Stuck upon the barr att the entrance of the harbour and is lost; as is one of the sloops".

Without the *Queen Anne's Revenge*, the *Adventure*, and several of the sloops, Blackbeard and his crew was now unable to effectively fight or flee from the incoming force of pirate hunters. Aware that he could not escape royal authority, he thus looked toward accepting a royal pardon. Recently, the Crown had announced that all pirates, on condition that they stop their piracy in the Atlantic, would be offered a pardon on or before September 5, 1718 for all crimes committed before January 5, 1718. Blackbeard, of course, had committed some significant crimes - including the blockade of Charleston - after that date, but he apparently thought he could successfully negotiate and receive a pardon.

According to David Herriot, it was Blackbeard's goal all along to intentionally scuttle his fleet and break up his crew, which now numbered over 300 pirates, and it is widely believed that Blackbeard had told Stede Bonnet that he intended to receive a pardon. By intentionally destroying his ships and forcing his crew to split up, Blackbeard also ensured that he and the men who remained with him on his old boat, the *Revenge*, would gain a bigger share of the booty.

To test the waters, Blackbeard sent Stede Bonnet to see the Royal Governor of North Carolina, Charles Eden, to petition for a pardon, figuring that if Bonnet came back alive it meant Blackbeard could also receive a pardon. This petition was successful, and Bonnet was granted a pardon for all crimes, including those that occurred after January in Charleston, but as he set back to return to the *Revenge*, Bonnet found that Blackbeard had removed everything of value from the ship and marooned its crew before moving on. Bonnet and those men aimed to find Blackbeard but never did, and when they went back to being pirates, they were captured in late September and hanged.

Aware of Bonnet's success in receiving a pardon, Blackbeard took his much reduced fleet and crew to an area off the mainland of North Carolina and had his remaining ships anchored. He now let the rest of his crew in on his plan to obtain a pardon, likely doing this at sea so that in the event that his crew protested, they could not disperse. They were forced to stay with him or swim to land. Once his crew knew of his intent to request a pardon and thus give up piracy, he moved on to Bath, North Carolina, arriving there just days after Bonnet had received his pardon. Days later, Blackbeard and his crew received a pardon from Royal Governor Eden in North Carolina.

Blackbeard now found himself in an unusual place: on land.

Chapter 6: The Return of Blackbeard

Blackbeard had allegedly confided in Bonnet that he wished to receive a pardon, and he had indeed, allowing him to transfer to civilian life. But it's widely believed that Blackbeard never actually intended to do so, and that obtaining the pardon was merely a ploy. Charles Johnson asserted, "Teach goes up to the Governor of North-Carolina, with about twenty of his Men, surrender to his Majesty's Proclamation, and receive Certificates thereof, from his Excellency; but it did not appear that their submitting to this Pardon was from any Reformation of Manners, but only to wait a more favourable Opportunity to play the same Game over again."

Whether that was accurate or not, Blackbeard did settle for a time in Bath, traveling frequently between the town and his sloop at sea. Charles Johnson wrote that Blackbeard even married the 16 year old daughter of a local plantation owner while in Bath, although no documents of any kind have been able to verify it. What is known is that Blackbeard stayed in Bath for the duration of July and through most of August, maintaining his sloop anchored near Ocracoke Island. At the time, Bath was an extremely small settlement with just a handful of families, but it had long been an important port city due to its access to the Atlantic Ocean. Bath, however, was slowly on the wane, and by 1718 it was losing business to other ports, including Charleston, which attracted significantly more commerce.

While Blackbeard stayed in Bath, his crew had largely moved on to areas outside of Bath and were all dispersing across the North American mainland. What became of them is unknown, but Blackbeard was now planning to return to the sea, and his timing was perfect because war was about to break out between Britain and Spain. It's possible if not likely that Blackbeard had anticipated war coming when he decided to "give up" piracy and receive a pardon.

In the summer of 1718, the same concept that had ignited Queen Anne's War - the Spanish Crown's desire to also control the French Crown - came to the fore again. The "Sun King", King Louis XIV of France, had died in 1715, and his only surviving grandson was King Philip V of Spain. However, the terms that ended Queen Anne's War - also known as the War of Spanish Succession - excluded Philip from inheriting the throne. The Treaty of Utrecht thus gave the throne to Louis' childhood great grandson, King Louis XV. A few years later, however, Philip, who was born in France and seemed originally to be the rightful heir to the French crown, wanted to reclaim what he believed was due to him and thus declared war on France. In return, France allied with Great Britain, the Holy Roman Empire, the Dutch Republic and Savoy to form what would later be called the Quadruple Alliance, which united against Spain.

When the fighting started, privateers were needed once again, so Blackbeard went to speak with Governor Eden about being given the chance to become a British privateer. For his part, Eden recognized the chance of removing a potentially troublesome pirate by allowing him to head to Saint Thomas to seek out a position as a privateer. Thus, Blackbeard sailed off away from Bath on a sloop he renamed the *Adventure*.

Blackbeard never reached Saint Thomas, almost certainly because Blackbeard never had any intention of going there and becoming a privateer. Instead, he simply decided to move slightly north along the North American coast and resumed his piracy against colonial ships. With that turn of events, people began to believe Governor Eden was an ally of the Atlantic pirates, taking note of the fact that North Carolina had attracted numerous pirates along its shores and many of them were sent off to "secure privateering positions". Like Blackbeard, however, most of the pirates never actually did become privateers, instead returning to piracy and using North Caroline as their base.

Indeed, historians have noted that Eden engaged in illegal trade with the pirates, and he was about to do so with Blackbeard. Rather than move towards the Caribbean with just one sloop, Blackbeard decided to stay along the North Carolinian, Virginian and Delaware Coasts, during which he raided two French ships that were shipping goods south to the Caribbean. Blackbeard moved one of the ships' crews to the other ship and stole one of the two ships, but when asked by Eden he claimed that he found the ship deserted, even though it was carrying a considerable amount of sugar. An admiralty court judged that the ship was found derelict, allowing the sugar to be apportioned to Eden and Blackbeard himself.

Other colonial leaders, however, were not so happy to share in the spoils. One such Governor was the Governor of Pennsylvania, who issued a warrant for Blackbeard's arrest in late 1718. This, however, was relatively ineffective. Though Blackbeard had operated in Delaware Bay, which touched Philadelphia, he did not routinely go there. Worse, he was stationed far off from Pennsylvania, in North Carolina, and the Pennsylvania Governor had no authority to make an arrest in North Carolinian waters. Though the Governor of Pennsylvania sent sloops out towards the southern colonies to capture and arrest Blackbeard, they failed to find or confront the famous pirate. So long as Blackbeard remained away from Delaware Bay, he would be safe.

In the meantime, Blackbeard continued to anchor around Ocracoke Inlet off the coast near Bath, where he could both rely on Governor Eden and see ships coming in and out from a distance. But other colonial governors outside of North Carolina were beginning to worry about the dreadful pirate off their coasts, including Governor Alexander Spotswood of nearby Virginia. Many North Carolina citizens had petitioned the Virginia Governor for assistance in finding Blackbeard, since they believed their own Governor was secretly allied with the pirate and would do nothing to end his terror. But since some of Blackbeard's crew had begun residing in small port towns along Virginia's coast, this gave Spotswood a motive to issue a proclamation of arrest for their captain.

Governor Spotswood

However, Spotswood had some legal issues to deal with. When he learned that one of Blackbeard's men, a pirate named William Howard, was in Virginia territory, Spotswood had Howard arrested, only to have Howard's lawyers claim the Governor had no authority to arrest, detain, and try him. Spotswood responded by citing a statute that he claimed allowed the Governor to arrest criminals without trial if the situation was deemed urgent enough.

The situation with piracy seemed urgent enough to make this argument compelling, and Howard was sentenced to hang, but when word arrived from London that the British wanted all captured pirates to be allowed a chance to receive a pardon and give up piracy before July 23, 1718, Howard was pardoned. But in the process of pardoning Howard, Spotswood was able to obtain important information from him about Blackbeard's whereabouts. Moreover, for those pirates who would not accept a pardon, the British Crown put a price on their head. In November 1718, a proclamation offered a sizable reward to anyone who could help capture or kill Blackbeard:

> "Whereas, by an Act of Assembly, made at a Session of Assembly, begun at the Capital in Williamsburgh, the eleventh Day of November, in the fifth Year of his

Majesty's Reign, entitled, An Act to encourage the apprehending and destroying of Pyrates: It is, amongst other Things enacted, that all and every Person, or Persons, who, from and after the fourteenth Day of November, in the Year of our Lord one thousand seven hundred and eighteen, and before the fourteenth Day of November, which shall be in the Year of our Lord one thousand seven hundred and nineteen, shall take any Pyrate, or Pyrates, on the Sea or Land, or in Case of Resistance, shall kill any such Pyrate…shall be entitled to have, and receive out of the publick Money, in the Hands of the Treasurer of this Colony, the several Rewards following; that is to say, for Edward Teach, commonly call'd Captain Teach, or Black-Beard, one hundred Pounds, for every other Commander of a Pyrate Ship, Sloop, or Vessel, forty Pounds…"

In addition to that, the Assembly of Virginia put a price on the capture of Blackbeard, and to help locate and capture or kill him, Governor Spotswood personally financed a mission headed by Lieutenant Robert Maynard to find the pirate off the coasts of North America. Some believe that Spotswood personally financed the mission in the hopes that the capture of Blackbeard would give him access to what he assumed would be a large horde of treasure, but whatever the motives Maynard took command of a small fleet on November 17, 1718 and set off to find Blackbeard. Maynard's two boats were named the *Jane* and *Ranger*, the last ironically sharing the name of Hornigold's pirate flagship in 1717.

On the evening of November 21, just days after beginning his search, Maynard found Blackbeard and his crew anchored off Ocracoke Inlet. Maynard had relied on information supplied by Howard, and this was Blackbeard's typical anchoring spot, so it was no surprise that Maynard found him there. Maynard went about preventing all traffic from entering or leaving the Ocracoke Inlet, but Blackbeard himself was entertaining guests on Ocracoke Island and was unaware Maynard had found him. Maynard had two ships and about 60 men, while Blackbeard had one sloop and about 25 men.

The following morning, Maynard saw Blackbeard aboard the *Adventure* and thus prepared to attack, but the element of surprise was lost. According to Charles Johnson, Blackbeard and Maynard engaged in legendary banter before the fight commenced:

"*Damn you for Villains, who are you? And, from whence came you?* The Lieutenant made him Answer, *You may see by our Colours we are no Pyrates. Black-beard* bid him send his Boat on Board, that he might see who he was; but Mr. *Maynard* reply'd thus; *I cannot spare my Boat, but I will come aboard of you as soon as I can, with my Sloop.* Upon this, *Black-beard* took a Glass of Liquor, and drank to him with these Words: *Damnation seize my Soul if I give you Quarters, or take any from you.* In Answer to which, Mr. *Maynard* told him, *That he expected no Quarters from him, nor should he give him any.*"

Once enemy ships came in range of the *Adventure*, it fired upon them, and Blackbeard maneuvered his sloop to bring his guns to bear against the *Ranger* and *Jane*. It's unclear whether the two sides fired guns at each other, but eventually they were in position to deliver broadside cannon attacks against each other. The broadsides on both sides delivered equally devastating results. Maynard would ultimately lose as much of a third of his men in the attack, and at some point, it's believed that shooting from Maynard's men destroyed the *Adventure*'s jib sheet, causing the crew to lose control of the sloop and have it run aground on a sandbar.

However it happened, Maynard's boats moved toward the *Adventure* until they came into contact, and Maynard had a trick up his sleeve. He kept many of his men below deck, anticipating early and damaging fire from Blackbeard, and the ruse worked. As the *Adventure* attacked the deck of Maynard's ships and found them empty, the confident pirates actually jumped off their own ship to board Maynard's. At that point, Maynard brought his men back on deck to counterattack, greatly surprising the pirates. The battle had now devolved into a one-on-one, man-on-man fight, complete with guns and swords.

While chaos ensued, Blackbeard and Maynard spotted each other and moved toward each other, engaging in a personal swordfight. But Maynard's men greatly outnumbered the pirates, and as Blackbeard tried to personally kill Maynard, he was slashed across the neck by one of Maynard's crew. Despite the severe wound, he continued until several of Maynard's men fell upon him and slashed and fired at him. Maynard later claimed Blackbeard had suffered five gunshot wounds and had been slashed at least 20 times.

"Here was an End of that couragious Brute, who might have pass'd in the World for a Heroe, had he been employ'd in a good Cause; his Destruction, which was of such Consequence to the Plantations, was entirely owing to the Conduct and Bravery of Lieutenant Maynard and his Men, who might have destroy'd him with much less Loss, had they had a Vessel with great Guns; but they were obliged to use small Vessels, because the Holes and Places he lurk'd in, would not admit of others of greater Draught; and it was no small Difficulty for this Gentleman to get to him, having grounded his Vessel, at least, a hundred times, in getting up the River, besides other Discouragements, enough to have turn'd back any Gentleman without Dishonour, who was less resolute and bold than this Lieutenant."

***Capture of the Pirate, Blackbeard, 1718*, a 1920 painting by Jean Leon Gerome Ferris**

Upon Blackbeard's death, his pirates mostly stopped fighting. History's most famous pirate had finally been stopped. With Maynard's men finally victorious, Blackbeard's corpse was beheaded, and his body was thrown into the Atlantic Ocean, an appropriate resting place. Somehow, a legend persisted that his headless body swam around his sloop three times before sinking, but his head was definitely attached to the mast of Maynard's ship so the Lieutenant could provide proof of Blackbeard's death and thus collect both the Royal and Virginia awards. Of the pirates taken prisoner, all but two of them were hanged along Williamsburg's Capitol Landing and left to rot, providing a gruesome sight that ensured the location became known as "Gallows Road". The two pirates who survived successfully claimed that they were only present because they had been guests of Blackbeard's at a drinking party held on the *Adventure* the night before. Charles Johnson added an ironic twist to the story of the battle, writing, "What seems a little odd, is, that some of these Men, who behaved so bravely against Black-beard, went afterwards a pyrating themselves..."

Governor Eden, meanwhile, was embarrassed and angry by the attack. Governor Spotswood of Virginia had conducted the raid in undeniably North Carolinian waters. But Eden's perceived support of the pirates had depleted any clout he had with the colonists of North Carolina - or the British Crown - and he was unable to pursue much protest. Moreover, Charles Johnson wrote that while rummagine Blackbeard's sloop, Maynard and his men found personal correspondence between Blackbeard and Eden onboard.

Illustration of Blackbeard's head, from Charles Elles's *The Pirates Own Book* (1837)

Chapter 7: Blackbeard's Legacy

"We normally think about pirates as sort of blood-lusting, that they want to slash somebody to pieces. A pirate, just like a normal person, would probably rather not have killed someone, but pirates knew that if that person resisted them and they didn't do something about it, their reputation and thus their brand name would be impaired. So you can imagine a pirate rather reluctantly engaging in this behavior as a way of preserving that reputation." - Peter Leeson

Among historians, the era in which Blackbeard lived and died, 1670-1720 is often called the "Golden Age of Piracy," and Blackbeard himself plays a central role in that designation. His death in 1718 comes very close to the semi-official "end" of the Golden Age, hardly by coincidence.

Starting with Spain in the early 1500's, a series of other countries - France, England and the Netherlands primarily - followed Spain's lead over a hundred years later and began colonizing distant parts of the world. Of course, because of the long distances required, naval supremacy was a central part of this imperial expansion. With life on the high seas came piracy. Blackbeard's area of control was the central place in the birth of Western piracy. French buccaneers began the trend by seizing Spanish ships in the area and stealing their goods and treasures.

Though the era of the Golden Age of Piracy was long and varied - French buccaneers were very different from their English counterparts - Blackbeard has come to be the symbolic face of all pirates of the era. The disheveled, swashbuckling, eccentric pirate is indeed the stereotypical image Westerners hold of the pirates of the era, and Blackbeard's ability to fascinate generations of people is largely responsible for the ongoing popularity of the pirates as a subject of interest.

Even shortly after his death, Blackbeard was recognized for his prominence in Charles Johnson's 1724 pirate history, which was published that year in England and chronicled Blackbeard's life. From then on, Edward Teach assumed a central role in the history of Western piracy. Among the people of the West, Blackbeard is invariably the first pirate that comes to mind, and sometimes the only pirate an individual can name.

Like any legendary and mysterious figure, numerous superstitions abound surrounding the life and death of Blackbeard. These are especially prominent, unsurprisingly, in North Carolina and Virginia, where Blackbeard's piracy was most prevalent in 1718. In other ways, Blackbeard lives on in the public imagination through a series of myths, many of which are unsubstantiated and reflect the scarcity of information known about the actual man.

Some of Blackbeard's quirky characteristics have been recorded, but historians remain unsure the extent to which they are true. The tale of Blackbeard wearing lit matches under his hat to give his face extra glow and make him appear as a figure emerging from a shroud of smoke is colorful, but whether it's true or not, it serves to explain that Blackbeard was a truly fearless pirate who would do anything to intimidate his opponents.

The idea of pirates burying treasure all over also has its origins in Blackbeard, thanks to Robert Louis Stevenson's *Treasure Island*, but Blackbeard was all too happy to sell or drink his treasure and had little interest in burying it, especially because most of it consisted of perishable goods. In fact, few pirates actually buried any treasure. They stole treasure, and burying it and leaving it vulnerable didn't exactly make sense for their purposes of making money and achieving wealth.

While Blackbeard is the most famous pirate ever, he has often been characterized and remembered as the "greatest pirate ever" or the most successful. On the contrary, Blackbeard was only most successful when it came to capturing the imagination of the British, and later the West. Blackbeard was a mildly successful pirate who was hardly the best of his generation; many French buccaneers had captured and looted more treasure than Blackbeard had.

Today, superstition continues to create myths around Blackbeard's character. Throughout Virginia and North Carolina, mysterious lights are often seen, and locals refer to them as "Teach's Lights."

Accounts of Blackbeard's life have been fused with modern media and poetic license to turn Blackbeard into the archetypal pirate in film and literature. Pirate "language" originates with impressions of Blackbeard, as do pirate costumes, but contrary to popular belief the stereotypical pirate accent is not Scotch or Scotch-Irish. Instead, it's of West Country English origin. The particular accent of Southwestern English was very similar to that portrayed as the "pirate accent" today. The reason for that is simple: Blackbeard hailed from Bristol, a port town in Southwest England. When researchers for modern films decided how to make Blackbeard sound, they looked first to his place of origin. They then studied the accent of 18th-century Bristol and discovered unique words like "arr" and "matey." With that, pirates were invariably depicted as sounding like someone from Blackbeard's home. This was obviously not the case, but the idea stuck with the general public, and it owes its origins directly to Blackbeard.

That's not the whole story, though. When trying to research what an accent sounded like in the 18th century, historians needed to use written materials, since voices had not been recorded back then. They thus encountered some significant amount of error. As such, the likely accent of Blackbeard, the one known to all posterity, is inaccurate. Written accounts do not dispel the various differences among social classes and occupations that would have existed and changed Blackbeard's accent. Thus, knowing what Blackbeard would have sounded like is impossible.

However inaccurate the instantly recognizable "pirate accent" may be, it demonstrates powerfully how central Blackbeard is to the history of piracy in the West, and especially in North America. His words, though created without much substantive evidence, continue to define the meaning of piracy today.

Numerous books and films have been created, with Blackbeard as their primary subject. These include both fictional and nonfictional accounts of Blackbeard's life. Film accounts of Blackbeard go back to some of the earliest films ever made. In the 1950's, *Blackbeard the Pirate* was created and many similar renditions have been made over the years. As recently as the late 2000's, the Hallmark channel aired a multipart series entitled *Blackbeard*. The piece drew many viewers.

300 years after his death, Blackbeard continues to occupy an important place in the West, literally. In addition to being commemorated and remembered through films, television, and books, his life and piracy have been commemorated by monuments constructed explicitly to his memory. Each year, the famed Ocracoke Island hosts a reenactment of Blackbeard's death that attracts hundreds of spectators, who come to enjoy the frivolity and drama of the event.

Similarly, historians and archeologists continue to be fascinated by the prospect of finding out more about Blackbeard, who led a life that is largely unknown to contemporary historians. The North Carolina Maritime Museum, located in Beaufort, has many objects believed to be associated with Blackbeard and his piracy. The biggest historical discovery pertaining to Blackbeard came in the late 1990's when maritime archaeologists discovered the shipwreck believed to be *Queen Anne's Revenge*. The discovery was made off Fort Macon State Park in North Carolina, in relatively shallow waters in the Atlantic Ocean, and that shipwreck was discovered by recreating historical accounts of the incident and using them to track down a possible location for the ship. Underwater video of the capturing of the ship was uploaded to the internet for educational purposes, and artifacts have been brought to shore, many of them lending further credence to the idea that the ship really is *Queen Anne's Revenge*. This includes the fact that the ship had loaded cannons on board at the time of its sinking. Though still undergoing excavation, the National Geographic Society has explicitly stated its belief that the ship is *Queen Anne's Revenge*, and it has been slated for underwater preservation.

Though hated by many in his time, Blackbeard continues to fascinate people across the globe 3 centuries after his piracy. Movies, films and historical discoveries capture the attention of thousands of people every year, while legends terrify them along the Atlantic Coast. Blackbeard lives on in powerful ways, creating a worldwide image of 18th century piracy through one man alone.

Blackbeard's Entry in *A General History of the Pyrates*

It has long been believed that *A General History of the Robberies and Murders of the most notorious Pyrates* was authored by Daniel Defoe under the alias "Captain Charles Johnson", but modern scholars have suggested other potential authors. As noted by pirate researcher Colin Woodard in his book *The Republic of Pirates*, "Recently, Arne Bialuschewski of the University of Kiel in Germany has identified a far more likely candidate: Nathaniel Mist, a former sailor, journalist, and publisher of the Weekly Journal. The book's first publisher of record, Charles Rivington, had printed many books for Mist, who lived just a few yards from his office. More importantly, the General History was registered at Her Majesty's Stationery Office in Mist's name. As a former seaman who had sailed the West Indies, Mist, of all London's writer-publishers, was uniquely qualified to have penned the book...Mist was also a committed

Jacobite...which could explain the General History's not entirely unsympathetic account of the maritime outlaws."

In fact, the sympathetic and overexaggerated nature of the author's profiles of various pirates is responsible for creating the lore that still surrounds pirates like Blackbeard today. The history is rife with anecdotes about pirates missing legs, burying treasure, missing eyes, and sailing aboard notorious ships like the Jolly Roger. While most of the profiles relied on the available facts, it was the artistic poetic license that has helped the history and its subjects endure.

One of those profiles, of course, was Blackbeard. The profile for Blackbeard is reproduced below:

Edward Teach was a Bristol Man born, but had sailed some Time out of Jamaica in Privateers, in the late French War; yet tho' he had often distinguished himself for his uncommon Boldness and personal Courage, he was never raised to any Command, till he went a-pyrating, which I think was at the latter End of the Year 1716, when Captain Benjamin Hornigold put him into a Sloop that he had made Prize of, and with whom he continued in Consortship till a little while before Hornigold surrendered.

In the Spring of the Year 1717, Teach and Hornigold sailed from Providence, for the Main of America, and took in their Way a Billop from the Havana, with 120 Barrels of Flower, as also a Sloop from Bermuda, Thurbar Master, from whom they took only some Gallons of Wine, and then let him go; and a Ship from Madera to South-Carolina, out of which they got Plunder to a considerable Value.

After cleaning on the Coast of Virginia, they returned to the West-Indies, and in the Latitude of 24, made Prize of a large French Guiney Man, bound to Martinico, which by Hornigold's Consent, Teach went aboard of as Captain, and took a Cruize in her; Hornigold returned with his Sloop to Providence, where, at the Arrival of Captain Rogers, the Governor, he surrendered to Mercy, pursuant to the King's Proclamation.

Aboard of this Guiney Man Teach mounted no Guns, and named her the Queen Ann's Revenge; and cruising near the Island of St. Vincent, took a large Ship, called the Great Allen, Christopher Taylor Commander; the Pyrates plundered her of what they though fit, put all the Men ashore upon the Island above mentioned, and then set Fire to the Ship.

A few Days after, Teach fell in with the Scarborogh Man of War, of 30 Guns, who engaged him for some Hours; but she finding the Pyrate well mann'd, and having tried her strength, gave over the Engagement, and returned to Barbadoes, the Place of her Station; and Teach sailed towards the Spanish America.

In his Way he met with a Pyrate Sloop of ten Guns, commanded by one Major Bonnet, lately a

Gentleman of good Reputation and Estate in the Island of Barbadoes, whom he joyned; but in a few Days after, Teach, finding that Bonnet knew nothing of a maritime Life, with the Consent of his own Men, put in another Captain, one Richards, to Command Bonnet's Sloop, and took the Major on aboard his own Ship, telling him, that as he had not been used to the Fatigues and Care of such a Post, it would be better for him to decline it, and live easy and at his Pleasure, in such a Ship as his, where he should not be obliged to perform Duty, but follow his own Inclinations.

At Turniff ten Leagues short of the Bay of Honduras, the Pyrates took in fresh Water; and while they were at an Anchor there, they saw a Sloop coming in, whereupon, Richards in the Sloop called the Revenge, slipped his Cable, and run out to meet her; who upon seeing the black Flag hoisted, struck his Sail and came to, under the Stern of Teach the Commadore. She was called the Adventure, from Jamaica, David Harriot Master. They took him and his Men aboard the great Ship, and sent a Number of other Hands with Israel Hands, Master of Teach's Ship, to Man the Sloop for the pyratical Account.

The 9th of April, they weighed from Turniff, having lain there about a Week, and sailed to the Bay, where they found a Ship and four Sloops, three of the latter belonged to Jonathan Bernard, of Jamaica, and the other to Captain James; the Ship was of Boston, called the Protestant Cæsar, Captain Wyar Commander. Teach hoisted his Black Colours, and fired a Gun, upon which Captain Wyar and all his Men, left their Ship, and got ashore in their Boat. Teach's Quarter-Master, and eight of his Crew, took Possession of Wyar's Ship, and Richards secured all the Sloops, one of which they burnt out of spight to the Owner; the Protestant Cæsar they also burnt, after they had plundered her, because she belonged to Boston, where some Men had been hanged for Pyracy; and the three Sloops belonging to Bernard they let go.

From hence the Rovers sailed to Turkill, and then to the Grand Caimanes, a small Island about thirty Leagues to the Westward of Jamaica, where they took a small Turtler, and so to the Havana, and from thence to the Bahama Wrecks, and from the Bahama Wrecks, they sailed to Carolina, taking a Brigantine and two Sloops in their Way, where they lay off the Bar of Charles-Town for five or six Days. They took here a Ship as she was coming out, bound for London, commanded by Robert Clark, with some Passengers on Board for England; the next Day they took another Vessel coming out of Charles-Town, and also two Pinks coming into Charles-Town; likewise a Brigantine with 14 Negroes aboard; all which being done in the Face of the Town, struck a great Terror to the whole Province of Carolina, having just before been visited by Vane, another notorious Pyrate, that they abandoned themselves to Dispair, being in no Condition to resist their Force. They were eight Sail in the Harbour, ready for the Sea, but none dared to venture out, it being almost impossible to escape their Hands. The inward bound Vessels were under the same unhappy Dilemma, so that the Trade of this Place was totally interrupted: What made these Misfortunes heavier to them, was a long expensive War, the Colony had had with the Natives, which was but just ended when these Robbers infested them.

Teach detained all the Ships and Prisoners, and, being in want of Medicines, resolves to demand a Chest from the Government of the Province; accordingly Richards, the Captain of the Revenge Sloop, with two or three more Pyrates, were sent up along with Mr. Marks, one of the Prisoners, whom they had taken in Clark's Ship, and very insolently made their Demands, threatning, that if they did not send immediately the Chest of Medicines, and let the Pyrate-Ambassadors return, without offering any Violence to their Persons, they would murder all their Prisoners, send up their Heads to the Governor, and set the Ships they had taken on Fire.

Whilst Mr. Marks was making Application to the Council, Richards, and the rest of the Pyrates, walk'd the Streets publickly, in the Sight of all People, who were fired with the utmost Indignation, looking upon them as Robbers and Murtherers, and particularly the Authors of their Wrongs and Oppressions, but durst not so much as think of executing their Revenge, for fear of bringing more Calamities upon themselves, and so they were forced to let the Villains pass with Impunity. The Government were not long in deliberating upon the Message, tho' 'twas the greatest Affront that could have been put upon them; yet for the saving so many Mens Lives, (among them, Mr. Samuel Wragg, one of the Council;) they comply'd with the Necessity, and sent aboard a Chest, valued at between 3 and 400 l. and the Pyrates went back safe to their Ships.

Blackbeard, (for so Teach was generally called, as we shall hereafter shew) as soon as he had received the Medicines and his Brother Rogues, let go the Ships and the Prisoners; having first taken out of them in Gold and Silver, about 1500 l. Sterling, besides Provisions and other Matters.

From the Bar of Charles-Town, they sailed to North-Carolina; Captain Teach in the Ship, which they called the Man of War, Captain Richards and Captain Hands in the Sloops, which they termed Privateers, and another Sloop serving them as a Tender. Teach began now to think of breaking up the Company, and securing the Money and the best of the Effects for himself, and some others of his Companions he had most Friendship for, and to cheat the rest: Accordingly, on Pretence of running into Topsail Inlet to clean, he grounded his Ship, and then, as if it had been done undesignedly, and by Accident; he orders Hands's Sloop to come to his Assistance, and get him off again, which he endeavouring to do, ran the Sloop on Shore near the other, and so were both lost. This done, Teach goes into the Tender Sloop, with forty Hands, and leaves the Revenge there; then takes seventeen others and Marroons them upon a small sandy Island, about a League from the Main, where there was neither Bird, Beast or Herb for their Subsistance, and where they must have perished if Major Bonnet had not two Days after taken them off.

Teach goes up to the Governor of North-Carolina, with about twenty of his Men, surrender to his Majesty's Proclamation, and receive Certificates thereof, from his Excellency; but it did not appear that their submitting to this Pardon was from any Reformation of Manners, but only to wait a more favourable Opportunity to play the same Game over again; which he soon after effected, with greater Security to himself, and with much better Prospect of Success, having in this Time cultivated a very good understanding with Charles Eden, Esq; the Governor above mentioned.

The first Piece of Service this kind Governor did to Black-Beard, was, to give him a Right to the Vessel which he had taken, when he was a pyrating in the great Ship called the Queen Ann's Revenge; for which purpose, a Court of Vice-Admiralty was held at Bath-Town; and, tho' Teach had never any Commission in his Life, and the Sloop belonging to the English Merchants, and taken in Time of Peace; yet was she condemned as a Prize taken from the Spaniards, by the said Teach. These Proceedings shew that Governors are but Men.

Before he sailed upon his Adventures, he marry'd a young Creature of about sixteen Years of Age, the Governor performing the Ceremony. As it is a Custom to marry here by a Priest, so it is there by a Magistrate; and this, I have been informed, made Teach's fourteenth Wife, whereof, about a dozen might be still living. His Behaviour in this State, was something extraordinary; for, while his Sloop lay in Okerecock Inlet, and he ashore at a Plantation, where his Wife lived, with whom after he had lain all Night, it was his Custom to invite five or six of his brutal Companions to come ashore, and he would force her to prostitute her self to them all, one after another, before his Face.

In June 1718, he went to Sea, upon another Expedition, and steered his Course towards Bermudas; he met with two or three English Vessels in his Way, but robbed them only of Provisions, Stores and other Necessaries, for his present Expence; but near the Island aforementioned, he fell in with two French Ships, one of them was loaden with Sugar and Cocoa, and the other light, both bound to Martinico; the Ship that had no Lading he let go, and putting all the Men of the loaded Ship aboard her, he brought home the other with her Cargo to North-Carolina, where the Governor and the Pyrates shared the Plunder.

When Teach and his Prize arrived, he and four of his Crew went to his Excellency, and made Affidavit, that they found the French Ship at Sea, without a Soul on Board her; and then a Court was called, and the Ship condemned: The Governor had sixty Hogsheads of Sugar for his Dividend, and one Mr. Knight, who was his Secretary, and Collector for the Province, twenty, and the rest was shared among the other Pyrates.

The Business was not yet done, the Ship remained, and it was possible one or other might come into the River, that might be acquainted with her, and so discover the Roguery; but Teach thought of a Contrivance to prevent this, for, upon a Pretence that she was leaky, and that she might sink, and so stop up the Mouth of the Inlet or Cove where she lay, he obtained an Order from the Governor, to bring her out into the River, and set her on Fire, which was accordingly executed, and she was burnt down to the Water's Edge, her Bottom sunk, and with it, their Fears of her ever rising in Judgment against them.

Captain Teach, alias Black-beard, passed three or four Months in the River, sometimes lying at

Anchor in the Coves, at other Times sailing from one Inlet to another, trading with such Sloops as he met, for the Plunder he had taken, and would often give them Presents for Stores and Provisions took from them; that is, when he happened to be in a giving Humour; at other Times he made bold with them, and took what he liked, without saying, by your Leave, knowing well, they dared not send him a Bill for the Payment. He often diverted himself with going ashore among the Planters, where he revelled Night and Day: By these he was well received, but whether out of Love or Fear, I cannot say; sometimes he used them courteously enough, and made them Presents of Rum and Sugar, in Recompence of what he took from them; but, as for Liberties (which 'tis said) he and his Companions often took with the Wives and Daughters of the Planters, I cannot take upon me to say, whether he paid them ad Valorem, or no. At other Times he carried it in a lordly Manner towards them, and would lay some of them under Contribution; nay, he often proceeded to bully the Governor, not, that I can discover the least Cause of Quarrel betwixt them, but it seemed only to be done, to shew he dared do it.

The Sloops trading up and down this River, being so frequently pillaged by Black-beard, consulted with the Traders, and some of the best of the Planters, what Course to take; they, saw plainly it would be in vain to make any Application to the Governor of North-Carolina, to whom it properly belonged to find some Redress; so that if they could not be relieved from some other Quarter, Black-beard would be like to reign with Impunity, therefore, with as much Secrecy as possible, they sent a Deputation to Virginia, to lay the Affair before the Governor of that Colony, and to solicit an armed Force from the Men of War lying there, to take or destroy this Pyrate.

This Governor consulted with the Captains of the two Men of War, viz. the Pearl and Lime, who had lain in St. James's River, about ten Months. It was agreed that the Governor should hire a couple of small Sloops, and the Men of War, should Man them; this was accordingly done, and the Command of them given to Mr. Robert Maynard, first Lieutenant of the Pearl, an experienced Officer, and a Gentleman of great Bravery and Resolution, as will appear by his gallant Behaviour in this Expedition. The Sloops were well mann'd and furnished with Ammunition and small Arms, but had no Guns mounted.

About the Time of their going out, the Governor called an Assembly, in which it was resolved to publish a Proclamation, offering certain Rewards to any Person or Persons, who, within a Year after that Time, should take or destroy any Pyrate: The original Proclamation being in our Hands, is as follows:

By his Majesty's Lieutenant Governor, and, Commander in Chief, of the Colony and Dominion of Virginia,

A PROCLAMATION,

Publishing the Rewards given for apprehending, or killing, Pyrates.

Whereas, by an Act of Assembly, made at a Session of Assembly, begun at the Capital in Williamsburgh, the eleventh Day of November, in the fifth Year of his Majesty's Reign, entituled, An Act to encourage the apprehending and destroying of Pyrates: It is, amongst other Things enacted, that all and every Person, or Persons, who, from and after the fourteenth Day of November, in the Year of our Lord one thousand seven hundred and eighteen, and before the fourteenth Day of November, which shall be in the Year of our Lord one thousand seven hundred and nineteen, shall take any Pyrate, or Pyrates, on the Sea or Land, or in Case of Resistance, shall kill any such Pyrate, or Pyrates, between the Degrees of thirty four, and thirty nine, of Northern Latitude, and within one hundred Leagues of the Continent of Virginia, or within the Provinces of Virginia, or North-Carolina, upon the Conviction, or making due Proof of the killing of all, and every such Pyrate, and Pyrates, before the Governor and Council, shall be entitled to have, and receive out of the publick Money, in the Hands of the Treasurer of this Colony, the several Rewards following; that is to say, for Edward Teach, commonly call'd Captain Teach, or Black-Beard, one hundred Pounds, for every other Commander of a Pyrate Ship, Sloop, or Vessel, forty Pounds; for every Lieutenant, Master, or Quarter-Master, Boatswain, or Carpenter, twenty Pounds; for every other inferior Officer, sixteen Pounds, and for every private Man taken on Board such Ship, Sloop, or Vessel, ten Pounds; and, that for every Pyrate, which shall be taken by any Ship, Sloop or Vessel, belonging to this Colony, or North-Carolina, within the Time aforesaid, in any Place whatsoever, the like Rewards shall be paid according to the Quality and Condition of such Pyrates. Wherefore, for the Encouragement of all such Persons as shall be willing to serve his Majesty, and their Country, in so just and honourable an Undertaking, as the suppressing a Sort of People, who may be truly called Enemies to Mankind: I have thought fit, with the Advice and Consent of his Majesty's Council, to issue this Proclamation, hereby declaring, the said Rewards shall be punctually and justly paid, in current Money of Virginia, according to the Directions of the said Act. And, I do order and appoint this Proclamation, to be published by the Sheriffs, at their respective County-Houses, and by all Ministers and Readers, in the several Churches and Chappels, throughout this Colony.

Given at our Council-Chamber at Williamsburgh, this 24th Day of November, 1718, in the fifth Year of his Majesty's Reign.

GOD SAVE THE KING.

A. SPOTSWOOD.

The 17th of November, 1718, the Lieutenant sail'd from Kicquetan, in James River in Virginia, and, the 21st in the Evening, came to the Mouth of Okerecock Inlet, where he got Sight of the Pyrate. This Expedition was made with all imaginable Secrecy, and the Officer manag'd with all the Prudence that was necessary, stopping all Boats and Vessels he met with, in the River, from going up, and thereby preventing any Intelligence from reaching Black-Beard, and receiving at the same time an Account from them all, of the Place where the Pyrate was lurking; but notwithstanding this Caution, Black-beard had Information of the Design, from his Excellency of the Province; and his Secretary, Mr. Knight, wrote him a Letter, particularly concerning it, intimating, That he had sent him four of his Men, which were all he could meet with, in or about Town, and so bid him be upon his Guard. These Men belonged to Black-beard, and were sent from Bath-Town to Okerecock Inlet, where the Sloop lay, which is about 20 Leagues.

Black-beard had heard several Reports, which happened not to be true, and so gave the less Credit to this, nor was he convinced till he saw the Sloops: Whereupon he put his Vessel in a Posture of Defence; he had no more than twenty five Men on Board, tho' he gave out to all the Vessels he spoke with, that he had 40. When he had prepared for Battle, he set down and spent the Night in drinking with the Master of a trading Sloop, who, 'twas thought, had more Business with Teach, than he should have had.

Lieutenant Maynard came to an Anchor, for the Place being shoal, and the Channel intricate, there was no getting in, where Teach lay, that Night; but in the Morning he weighed, and sent his Boat a-head of the Sloops to sound; and coming within Gun-Shot of the Pyrate, received his Fire; whereupon Maynard hoisted the King's Colours, and stood directly towards him, with the best Way that his Sails and Oars could made. Black-beard cut his Cable, and endeavoured to make a running Fight, keeping a continual Fire at his Enemies, with his Guns; Mr. Maynard not having any, kept a constant Fire with small Arms, while some of his Men laboured at their Oars. In a little Time Teach's Sloop ran a-ground, and Mr. Maynard's drawing more Water than that of the Pyrate, he could not come near him; so he anchored within half Gun-Shot of the Enemy, and, in order to lighten his Vessel, that he might run him aboard, the Lieutenant ordered all his Ballast to be thrown over-board, and all the Water to be staved, and then weigh'd and stood for him; upon which Black-beard hail'd him in this rude Manner: Damn you for Villains, who are you? And, from whence came you? The Lieutenant made him Answer, You may see by our Colours we are no Pyrates. Black-beard bid him send his Boat on Board, that he might see who he was; but Mr. Maynard reply'd thus; I cannot spare my Boat, but I will come aboard of you as soon as I can, with my Sloop. Upon this, Black-beard took a Glass of Liquor, and drank to him with these Words: Damnation seize my Soul if I give you Quarters, or take any from you. In Answer to which, Mr. Maynard told him, That he expected no Quarters from him, nor should he give him any.

By this time Black-beard's Sloop fleeted, as Mr. Maynard's Sloops were rowing towards him, which being not above a Foot high in the Waste, and consequently the Men all exposed, as they came near together, (there being hitherto little or no Execution done, on either Side,) the Pyrate fired a Broadside, charged with all Manner of small Shot. ——A fatal Stroke to them! The Sloop the Lieutenant was in, having twenty Men killed and wounded, and the other Sloop nine. This could not be help'd, for there being no Wind, they were oblig'd to keep to their Oars, otherwise the Pyrate would have got away from him, which, it seems, the Lieutenant was resolute to prevent.

After this unlucky Blow, Black-beard's Sloop fell Broadside to the Shore; Mr. Maynard's other Sloop, which was called the Ranger, fell a-stern, being, for the present, disabled; so the Lieutenant finding his own Sloop had Way, and would soon be on Board of Teach, he ordered all his Men down, for fear of another Broadside, which must have been their Destruction, and the loss of their Expedition. Mr. Maynard was the only Person that kept the Deck, except the Man at the Helm, whom he directed to lye down snug, and the Men in the Hold were ordered to get their Pistols and their Swords ready for close fighting, and to come up at his Command; in order to which, two Ladders were placed in the Hatch-Way for the more Expedition. When the Lieutenant's Sloop boarded the other, Captain Teach's Men threw in several new fashioned sort of Grenadoes, viz. Case Bottles fill'd with Powder, and small Shot, Slugs, and Pieces of Lead or Iron, with a quick Match in the Mouth of it, which being lighted without Side, presently runs into the Bottle to the Powder, and as it is instantly thrown on Board, generally does great Execution, besides putting all the Crew into a Confusion; but by good Providence, they had not that Effect here; the Men being in the Hold, and Black-beard seeing few or no Hands aboard, told his Men, That they were all knock'd on the Head, except three or four; and therefore, says he, let's jump on Board, and cut them to Pieces.

Whereupon, under the Smoak of one of the Bottles just mentioned, Black-beard enters with fourteen Men, over the Bows of Maynard's Sloop, and were not seen by him till the Air cleared; however, he just then gave a Signal to his Men, who all rose in an Instant, and attack'd the Pyrates with as much Bravery as ever was done upon such an Occasion: Black-beard and the Lieutenant fired the first Pistol at each other, by which the Pyrate received a Wound, and then engaged with Swords, till the Lieutenant's unluckily broke, and stepping back to cock a Pistol, Black-beard, with his Cutlash, was striking at that Instant, that one of Maynard's Men gave him a terrible Wound in the Neck and Throat, by which the Lieutenant came off with a small Cut over his Fingers.

They were now closely and warmly engaged, the Lieutenant and twelve Men, against Black-beard and fourteen, till the Sea was tinctur'd with Blood round the Vessel; Black-beard received a Shot into his Body from the Pistol that Lieutenant Maynard discharg'd, yet he stood his Ground, and fought with great Fury, till he received five and twenty Wounds, and five of them by Shot. At length, as he was cocking another Pistol, having fired several before, he fell down dead; by which Time eight more out of the fourteen dropp'd, and all the rest, much wounded, jump'd over-board, and call'd out for Quarters, which was granted, tho' it was only prolonging their Lives for a few Days. The Sloop Ranger came up, and attack'd the Men that remain'd in Black-beard's Sloop, with equal Bravery, till they likewise cry'd for Quarters.

Here was an End of that couragious Brute, who might have pass'd in the World for a Heroe, had he been employ'd in a good Cause; his Destruction, which was of such Consequence to the Plantations, was entirely owing to the Conduct and Bravery of Lieutenant Maynard and his Men, who might have destroy'd him with much less Loss, had they had a Vessel with great Guns; but they were obliged to use small Vessels, because the Holes and Places he lurk'd in, would not admit of others of greater Draught; and it was no small Difficulty for this Gentleman to get to him, having grounded his Vessel, at least, a hundred times, in getting up the River, besides other Discouragements, enough to have turn'd back any Gentleman without Dishonour, who was less resolute and bold than this Lieutenant. The Broadside that did so much Mischief before they boarded, in all Probability saved the rest from Destruction; for before that Teach had little or no Hopes of escaping, and therefore had posted a resolute Fellow, a Negroe whom he had bred up, with a lighted Match, in the Powder-Room, with Commands to blow up when he should give him Orders, which was as soon as the Lieutenant and his Men could have entered, that so he might have destroy'd his Conquerors: and when the Negro found how it went with Black-beard, he could hardly be perswaded from the rash Action, by two Prisoners that were then in the Hold of the Sloop.

What seems a little odd, is, that some of these Men, who behaved so bravely against Black-beard, went afterwards a pyrating themselves, and one of them was taken along with Roberts; but I do not find that any of them were provided for, except one that was hanged; but this is a Digression.

The Lieutenant caused Black-beard's Head to be severed from his Body, and hung up at the Bolt-sprit End, then he sailed to Bath-Town, to get Relief for his wounded Men.

It must be observed, that in rummaging the Pyrate's Sloop, they found several Letters and written Papers, which discovered the Correspondence betwixt Governor Eden, the Secretary and Collector, and also some Traders at New-York, and Black-beard. It is likely he had Regard enough for his Friends, to have destroyed these Papers before the Action, in order to hinder them from falling into such Hands, where the Discovery would be of no Use, either to the Interest or Reputation of these fine Gentlemen, if it had not been his fixed Resolution to have blown up together, when he found no possibility of escaping.

When the Lieutenant came to Bath-Town, he made bold to seize in the Governor's Store-House, the sixty Hogsheads of Sugar, and from honest Mr. Knight, twenty; which it seems was their Dividend of the Plunder taken in the French Ship; the latter did not long survive this shameful Discovery, for being apprehensive that he might be called to an Account for these Trifles, fell sick with the Fright, and died in a few Days.

After the wounded Men were pretty well recover'd, the Lieutenant sailed back to the Men of War in James River, in Virginia, with Black-beard's Head still hanging at the Bolt-sprit End, and fiveteen Prisoners, thirteen of whom were hanged. It appearing upon Tryal, that one of them, viz. Samuel Odell, was taken out of the trading Sloop, but the Night before the Engagement. This poor Fellow was a little unlucky at his first entering upon his new Trade, there appearing no less than 70 Wounds upon him after the Action, notwithstanding which, he lived, and was cured of them all. The other Person that escaped the Gallows, was one Israel Hands, the Master of Black-beard's Sloop, and formerly Captain of the same, before the Queen Ann's Revenge was lost in Topsail Inlet.

The aforesaid Hands happened not to be in the Fight, but was taken afterwards ashore at Bath-Town, having been sometime before disabled by Black-beard, in one of his savage Humours, after the following Manner.—One Night drinking in his Cabin with Hands, the Pilot, and another Man; Black-beard without any Provocation privately draws out a small Pair of Pistols, and cocks them under the Table, which being perceived by the Man, he withdrew and went upon Deck, leaving Hands, the Pilot, and the Captain together. When the Pistols were ready, he blew out the Candle, and crossing his Hands, discharged them at his Company; Hands, the Master, was shot thro' the Knee, and lam'd for Life; the other Pistol did no Execution. —Being asked the meaning of this, he only answered, by damning them, that if he did not now and then kill one of them, they would forget who he was.

Hands being taken, was try'd and condemned, but just as he was about to be executed, a Ship arrives at Virginia with a Proclamation for prolonging the Time of his Majesty's Pardon, to such of the Pyrates as should surrender by a limited Time therein expressed: Notwithstanding the Sentence, Hands pleaded the Pardon, and was allowed the Benefit of it, and is alive at this Time in London, begging his Bread.

Now that we have given some Account of Teach's Life and Actions, it will not be amiss, that we speak of his Beard, since it did not a little contribute towards making his Name so terrible in those Parts.

Plutarch, and other grave Historians have taken Notice, that several great Men amongst the Romans, took their Sir-Names from certain odd Marks in their Countenances; as Cicero, from a Mark or Vetch on his Nose; so our Heroe, Captain Teach, assumed the Cognomen of Black-beard, from that large Quantity of Hair, which, like a frightful Meteor, covered his whole Face, and frightened America more than any Comet that has appeared there a long Time.

This Beard was black, which he suffered to grow of an extravagant Length; as to Breadth, it came up to his Eyes; he was accustomed to twist it with Ribbons, in small Tails, after the Manner of our Ramilies Wiggs, and turn them about his Ears: In Time of Action, he wore a Sling over his Shoulders, with three brace of Pistols, hanging in Holsters like Bandaliers; and stuck lighted Matches under his Hat, which appearing on each Side of his Face, his Eyes naturally looking fierce and wild, made him altogether such a Figure, that Imagination cannot form an Idea of a Fury, from Hell, to look more frightful.

If he had the look of a Fury, his Humours and Passions were suitable to it; we shall relate two or three more of his Extravagancies, which we omitted in the Body of his History, by which it will appear, to what a Pitch of Wickedness, human Nature may arrive, if it's Passions are not checked.

In the Commonwealth of Pyrates, he who goes the greatest Length of Wickedness, is looked upon with a kind of Envy amongst them, as a Person of a more extraordinary Gallantry, and is thereby entitled to be distinguished by some Post, and if such a one has but Courage, he must certainly be a great Man. The Hero of whom we are writing, was thoroughly accomplished this Way, and some of his Frolicks of Wickedness, were so extravagant, as if he aimed at making his Men believe he was a Devil incarnate; for being one Day at Sea, and a little flushed with drink:—Come, says he, let us make a Hell of our own, and try how long we can bear it; accordingly he, with two or three others, went down into the Hold, and closing up all the Hatches, filled several Pots full of Brimstone, and other combustible Matter, and set it on Fire, and so continued till they were almost suffocated, when some of the Men cried out for Air; at length he opened the Hatches, not a little pleased that he held out the longest.

The Night before he was killed, he set up and drank till the Morning, with some of his own Men, and the Master of a Merchant-Man, and having had Intelligence of the two Sloops coming to attack him, as has been before observed; one of his Men asked him, in Case any thing should happen to him in the Engagement with the Sloops, whether his Wife knew where he had buried his Money? He answered, That no Body but himself and the Devil, knew where it was, and the longest Liver should take all.

Those of his Crew who were taken alive, told a Story which may appear a little incredible; however, we think it will not be fair to omit it, since we had it from their own Mouths. That once upon a Cruize, they found out that they had a Man on Board more than their Crew; such a one was seen several Days amongst them, sometimes below, and sometimes upon Deck, yet no Man in the Ship could give an Account who he was, or from whence he came; but that he disappeared little before they were cast away in their great Ship, but, it seems, they verily believed it was the Devil.

One would think these Things should induce them to reform their Lives, but so many Reprobates together, encouraged and spirited one another up in their Wickedness, to which a continual Course of drinking did not a little contribute; for in Black-beard's Journal, which was taken, there were several Memorandums of the following Nature, sound writ with his own Hand.— Such a Day, Rum all out:—Our Company somewhat sober:—A damn'd Confusion amongst us!—Rogues a plotting;—great Talk of Separation.—So I look'd sharp for a Prize;—such a Day took one, with a great deal of Liquor on Board, so kept the Company hot, damned hot, then all Things went well again.

Thus it was these Wretches passed their Lives, with very little Pleasure or Satisfaction, in the Possession of what they violently take away from others, and sure to pay for it at last, by an ignominious Death.

The Names of the Pyrates killed in the Engagement, are as follow.

Edward Teach, Commander.

Phillip Morton, Gunner.

Garrat Gibbens, Boatswain.

Owen Roberts, Carpenter.

Thomas Miller, Quarter-Master.

John Husk,

Joseph Curtice,

Joseph Brooks,

Nath. Jackson.

All the rest, except the two last, were wounded and afterwards hanged in Virginia.

John Carnes, Joseph Philips,

Joseph Brooks, James Robbins,

James Blake, John Martin,

John Gills, Edward Salter,

Thomas Gates, Stephen Daniel,

James White, Richard Greensail.

Richard Stiles, Israel Hands, pardoned.

Cæsar, Samuel Odel, acquited.

There were in the Pyrate Sloops, and ashore in a Tent, near where the Sloops lay, 25 Hogsheads of Sugar, 11 Teirces, and 145 Bags of Cocoa, a Barrel of Indigo, and a Bale of

Cotton; which, with what was taken from the Governor and Secretary, and the Sale of the Sloop, came to 2500 l. besides the Rewards paid by the Governor of Virginia, pursuant to his Proclamation; all which was divided among the Companies of the two Ships, Lime and Pearl, that lay in James River; the brave Fellows that took them coming in for no more than their Dividend amongst the rest, and was paid it within these three Months.